THE TUSCARORAS

The Tuscaroras

by Shirley Hill Witt

Crowell-Collier Press, New York, New York
COLLIER-MACMILLAN LTD., LONDON

The author and publisher wish to acknowledge
the contribution of Stan Steiner in
making this book possible.

For Tracy Lee Rickard

Contents

1.	The Lands	1

2.	The Christians	6

3.	The Great Peace	12

4.	The League	20

5.	The Islands	24

6.	The Border Crossing	29

7.	The Long House	33

8.	The Steelworkers	43

9.	The Ongwe Onwe	48

From a certain kind of shell found along the Atlantic seaboard, white and purple beads called wampum were made which could be strung and woven into belts. The Iroquois use these wampum belts in public affairs to mark the making of alliances and treaties, to record important political and religious events, and to formally present proposals from one people to another. The belts also serve as direct messages, as when a war belt was sent from nation to nation, or as a method where beads placed in certain ways can recall to mind complicated ritual that must be recited with complete accuracy. The Iroquois seek the return of their lost belts because the belts hold our history.

Some of the more important belts are drawn at the chapter openings of this book. A good and true friend of *Ongwe onwe* has helped us tell about the belts. *Niaweh,* Aren Akweks—Ray Fadden.

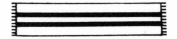

1. The Lands

We are called the Tuscaroras. We call ourselves *Skaroo'ren.* It means "the hemp gatherers." The two names are the same, just said a little differently.

We think our land is very beautiful. Until a few years ago, we had over six thousand acres near Niagara Falls, New York. The Tuscarora Reserve lies along the top of a ridge which falls away to another plain and then to the river. Most of our land is south of the drop-off, on rolling meadows, fields, and woods. The land that is ours below the ridge is mostly woodland and there is a spring, Black-nose Spring.

It seems that because we are near the east end of Lake Erie, we get a lot of snow. There is snow at the Tuscarora Reserve even when there is none east of us. The sky starts snowing early in October and there are snowstorms even late into April.

The snow gets deep sometimes and will drift in high dunes at the edges of fields. The deer come in closer to the houses then, looking for something to eat. We always leave some ears of corn on the stalks for them at harvest time. We know they will have trouble finding food in the deep snows.

But also the young men hunt the deer. The Tuscaroras must eat, too. And, of course, venison is the best of all meat. So we think.

One should take the bucks although the does taste better. The does must live so that they may drop their fawns in the springtime.

Other animal tribes are hunted in addition to deer: raccoon, rabbit, partridge, pheasant, geese, ducks. The young men go down to the river and spear sturgeon sometimes. A sturgeon is so big that we either give much of it away to other families or else freeze part of it for later. Once in a while the Algonkian Indians from Canada bring us moose. Or our men go there to hunt moose and elk.

When springtime comes, wherever you look it is so green that your eyes hurt. Then it is time to turn over the fields and get them ready for planting. Flowers appear on the dogwood trees in the woods. In the orchards, the fruit trees push out their flowers, too.

Not everybody farms on the Tuscarora Reserve. But those who do farm use not only their own fields but lands that they rent or borrow from other families also. Therefore, much of the Reserve is farmland. Woods and farmland. And hayfields.

The ancient Iroquois corn, beans, and squash—the Three Sisters—are still grown, and these taste the best.

So we think. But other crops and modern varieties are grown, too: tomatoes, green peppers, pumpkins, cucumbers, lettuce, spinach, kale, potatoes, and other things. Apples and grapes grow well and you will see orchards here and there. Peaches, too, and cherries.

Some people have tractors, harvesters, and other farm equipment. Others borrow these things when they need them.

The growing season is short but the summers are hot enough to ripen the plants quickly. The weeds have to be kept out of the fields, and that is the job for the children to do. Pulling weeds is hard work, though, and very boring—especially in the hot sun. But you can eat what you want.

In the autumn, the harvest must be brought in quickly, before the frost falls. People work together to bring it in. The haying gets done earlier, sometimes twice, if it is a good year. Autumn is when the butchering gets done, too; maybe a cow and some pigs, chickens, and ducks.

When the leaves falling from trees are red and yellow, when the harvest is in, we have corn-husking bees. A corn-husking bee is a party and everyone is invited. It is good to dress with many layers because the barn is not very warm at first. But with a lot of people husking corn, the work gives heat to the bodies and the bodies give heat to the barn.

To husk the corn for braiding, you hold the ear of corn in your left hand and, with your right hand, pull the leaves, or husks, down, making a tail on the ear. Just some of the husks should be pulled all the way off. About six or eight strong husks should be left on so that the tail can be braided in with other tails. Those who have good hands for braiding make long strings of corn that way. The braids are hung over big wooden beams so the ears will dry during the winter inside the barn.

The ones who are husking the corn play a game. The modern corn has yellow kernels and the ancient Iroquois corn has white kernels. But once in a while either kind of corn has a few red or blue or spotted kernels in its ear. If a boy gets an ear with colored kernels, he can kiss any girl he wants to. But if a girl gets an ear like that, she can hit any boy she wants to. There is much laughing and running around. You can tell who the sweethearts are. The old people do not play the game but they husk and braid and smile and laugh. The children run around jumping in the hayloft and playing games.

Squash and pumpkins are put away for the winter, too. They are sliced across, making circles, and are hung on pegs where they will dry with the corn during the winter.

The hay in the barn smells sweet at harvest time. It has just been mowed and brought in. The horses and cows are fat from it and from the good summer. The horses stomp around in their stalls, crunching on the hay that the children are holding for them.

Some people do not have barns since they are not farmers. But those with barns usually have a dooryard between the barn and the house. It is a sort of parking lot for cars and tractors and trucks. It is also where the chickens, ducks, geese, and dogs hang around. There are houses or pens for these birds and animals, but during the day they patrol the dooryard. Sometimes the chickens and the ducks get penned up. The chickens do not mind much but the ducks do. They discuss their capture and make an awful racket. They want to come and go as they please.

It is really the geese who think they own the dooryard. They honk when anybody drives in, just like watchdogs. They march over to the car or truck and check out the newcomers. If they are friends, the geese waddle away mumbling to themselves. If the visitors are strangers or people they do not like, they hiss like snakes and chase them, and may even give them a nip. You never forget a nip from a goose. And they run pretty fast, too, beating their wide wings as they charge.

Cats hang around in and out of the house. In the house, they sleep near the woodstove.

Farmhouses come in all sizes, but there is always a big dining table, no matter what. Even the houses owned by those who do not farm always have big tables.

That is because the Tuscaroras are very friendly. It is a rule that everyone who comes to the door must be fed, whether friend or stranger—and even if not hungry.

It is a Tuscarora belief that every so often the Creator tests our hospitality. The Creator will come to our houses wearing someone's body—it may be the body of a friend or of a stranger—and sees if we give friendship and food. Since we have no idea when or in what body the Creator will come, we welcome and feed everyone who comes to our door.

That is how Tuscaroras have learned to be very friendly.

Sometimes, being friendly has hurt the Tuscaroras.

War Belt · When this belt was sent out by the Confederacy, it was a declaration of war. If it returned with a string of white wampum, peace was declared. The figure represents a tomahawk. Holder: Buffalo and Erie County Historical Society

2. The Christians

We have not always lived in New York State and in Ontario, Canada. The Tuscarora homeland is in what is now called North Carolina.

When the white man invaded our country, Tuscarora lands extended from near the Atlantic seacoast clear inland to the Appalachian Mountains. Our hunters ranged even farther: the hunting lands extended into South Carolina and Virginia and even as far as Pennsylvania sometimes.

Thousands of Tuscarora people lived there then, in North Carolina. Five or six thousand, perhaps. There were larger and smaller settlements, ringed around by cornfields. The larger settlements were called "towns" by the white men when they saw them. So they must have been fairly good-sized places, considering it was the seventeenth century.

The villages and towns were made up of long houses. These were structures shaped somewhat like a very long loaf of bread. The inside was divided into several family apartments, each with its own fire, cooking area, beds, storage, and so forth.

Each long house was owned by a clan or part of a clan. All the women and all the children of the women were of the same clan and therefore related to each other. Only the husbands of the women were unrelated and from different clans. Their relationship was that of being husbands and fathers, but their clan and its women were of a different long house. When a man and woman married each other, they went to live in the long house of the wife's mother. That is how the women wove the long house together.

The settlements often had high fences or palisades surrounding them to protect the people from the enemy. When the enemy was another Indian tribe, the warriors and the palisades fairly well kept them away. But when the Christians came in with guns and cannons against us, with only our bows and arrows, well, that was different.

The books say that our first war with the Christians happened because we captured a surveyor and a German baron. But that does not make sense. Who needs a surveyor and a German baron? The Tuscaroras have always believed in peace. There must have been a reason for our capturing them. Something must have happened before we did that. In fact, lots of things must have happened.

Our old men—the ones who remember what their grandfathers told them—they tell us what the books do not say. They tell us how the Christians came in and wanted our lands. We pitied them. They must have been very unhappy in their countries in Europe to come so far. Why else would they come to our country?

The Tuscaroras felt sorry for these orphans. So, right away, we shared some land with them, a good piece of land—large enough for them to live on and to raise their crops.

But it seems that a Christian is never satisfied. He is never at peace with himself or with others. He always wants more and more and more. So it seems. And we gave those Europeans some more land and more land.

But the land they really wanted was our fields where we planted our crops. Our women turned the earth with digging sticks and hoes and coaxed Mother Earth to send up food for us. This She did. But She made us work hard for it.

And where we had worked hard, those were the lands that the white man wanted.

And that is not all. The Christians wanted slaves. They wanted us to be their slaves. We did not even know what a slave was until they came. And then we saw. And we were very unhappy.

It is not right to take people from their families, we thought. It is not right to make people do all the work and get nothing for their labor, we thought. It is not right to put iron chains on people and to whip them like dogs, we thought.

But that is what those Christians did.

At first, we pitied them. They had no homes, no lands.

Their tribes were far away. We gave them lands, we fed them, and we showed them how to coax Mother Earth.

But then they stole. They stole our lands and they stole our people. Our people that they stole were made into slaves. And they did not even keep the slaves, lots of times. They sold our people to other strangers who took them far away from our country. They herded them away like they did their cattle. Or they put them on big ships and sent them over the water to places we did not know.

So we tried to stop them. We at last had to fight them. We knew our people could not be slaves. They would die. We knew we had to keep our lands for food. Or we would die.

So we fought them.

Sometimes we won. Sometimes they won. Sometimes we tried to reason with them. One time we sent them Peace Belts of white and purple wampum shells. We sent them eight belts.

The first belt was sent by the elder women and mothers who asked for friendship with the Christian people so that they could fetch wood and water without risk or danger.

The second belt was sent for our children and our children yet to be born, asking that they be allowed to run and play without fear of death or slavery.

The young men sent the third belt. They needed to be free of the threat of death or slavery in order to go out and hunt meat for their mothers, their children, and the aged ones.

The old men, our wise elders, sent the fourth belt to the

Christians. They sought a long and lasting peace, so all men could walk the forests without fear.

All the Tuscaroras sent the fifth belt, asking the Christian people to be peaceful.

Our chiefs passed along the sixth belt seeking peace because the minds of the Tuscarora people had too long been uneasy with fear and anxiety.

The seventh belt said that the Christians should stop murdering people and enslaving them so that the Tuscarora would no longer have to fear all the sounds of the forest, even the mouse and the wind ruffling the leaves.

By the eighth belt, the Tuscarora people sought open communication and continuing communication with the Christians.

Nothing worked. The wars grew worse. There were more wars and more wars. The English, the Swiss, and the Germans all fought against us, all of them wanting land and slaves.

Lots of evil things happened. We killed and they killed. Peace was impossible.

And, at last, they won. Or, it should be said, our choice was either to be wiped from the breast of Mother Earth or to leave our beloved homeland, the few of us that were left.

So, with tears on our faces, we left the fields and forests where we had always lived. For more than two and a half centuries we have been cut away from our homeland.

In the north country we had strong and powerful relatives: the Five Nations of the Iroquois. They took us in, like orphaned children.

The Oneida Nation adopted us and gave us land on which to live and grow our crops.

But it was too soon for peace to come to us. The French and the British, and, later, the new nation of the United States came and killed our people. For more than a hundred years, for more than a century, our Tuscarora people knew not what peace was. But we kept looking for it.

It is not pleasant to recall and live with the tribal memories of those war-filled days. But our old men—the wise ones—make sure we do not forget. They say it is important to remember these things because it keeps us strong for now and in times to come.

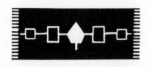

Hayontawatha Belt · Representing the Great Peace Compact of the first five Nations of the League, the square figures show the people and territory of the Seneca, Cayuga, Oneida, and Mohawk Nations. The heart or pine tree represents the Onondaga land and people where the Council Fire of the Great Peace is kindled. Holder: New York State Museum at Albany

3. The Great Peace

Now it is time to tell of the League of the Iroquois.

When the Algonkian tribes in the Northeast talked about the "Iroquois," their word for "enemies" or "rattlesnakes," they meant the large number of nations who lived in the center of Algonkian territory. A long time ago, that whole region had belonged to the Algonkians. But then—still in a time before man's memory begins—the Iroquois people came into the Algonkian forests and claimed a large middle section of it for themselves. Iroquois lands centered upon what is now called the St. Lawrence River, in what is now Canada and the United States.

Surrounded by Algonkians, the Iroquois had to fight

almost all the time to keep themselves and their colonies alive. The reason the Iroquois came into this hostile land and fought to keep it was because their legends told them that this was what they must do. The ancient stories say that the Creator directed them and led them into these new lands. It is much like the way that Yahweh led the ancient Hebrews to their new homelands.

The several Iroquois nations all spoke similar languages, languages very different from that of the Algonkian. Thus the Algonkians lumped them together and called them all "rattlesnakes."

But there were several nations and even though they were born together long ago and spoke similar languages, they were not especially friendly with each other. Even though they were enclosed by strong Algonkian enemies, that did not stop the Iroquois nations from fighting with one another. It seemed that they were constantly at war: with each other or with the Algonkians. It was a bad time for the Iroquois.

One day several hundred years ago—long before the Christians came to these shores—a strange and wonderful man was born among the Huron people. His mother dreamed that she would bear a son different from all other men. She was told in the dream to name her son "Dekanawida." This woman had no husband: Dekanawida was of virgin birth, just as Jesus of Nazareth.

When the son was born, his grandmother was ashamed of him and she told the mother to destroy him. Twice the mother chopped a hole in the ice of the river and threw the baby into the deeps. But each night, the baby would appear at her side, ready to be nursed. The third time, the grandmother threw him away. But, again, at nightfall, the baby had returned; they did not know how. So the grandmother said that, surely, this child must be a remarkable and important person. Thereafter, she and the mother took proper care of him.

The mother's dream had told her that Dekanawida should leave the Huron people and go to live among the People of the Flint, the Mohawks, and that he would one day go among the Many Hill People, the Onondaga, and raise up the Tree of Peace.

Dekanawida grew to be a man. The Hurons did not like him because he hated war and killing. So, one day he left the Hurons and went by canoe across Lake Ontario to the land of the Mohawks.

He made camp and then sat smoking a pipe under a tree. The Mohawks discovered him and they asked him questions, once they found out he had no weapons. They asked him why he had come to them.

Dekanawida said to them, "The Creator from whom we are all descended sent me to establish the Great Peace among you. No longer shall you kill one another and nations shall cease warring upon each other. Such things are entirely evil and your Maker forbids it. Peace and comfort are better than war and misery for a nation's welfare."

The Mohawks could not deny the truth that this man spoke. But they needed proof that he really did have special power to establish the Great Peace.

Dekanawida and the Mohawks went to a place where

the river broke and fell into a deep gorge. Leaning over the head of the falls was a tall tree. Dekanawida climbed up to its thin top branches. The Mohawks chopped the tree down. The tree and Dekanawida crashed into the roaring waters and were swept over the falls down into the thundering gorge far below.

The Mohawks went home. They were sure Dekanawida was dead. No man had power enough to bring the Great Peace, they thought. This Dekanawida had no power from the Creator, they thought.

The next morning, the Mohawk village was surprised to see smoke rising from the smoke hole of an empty house. They looked, and Dekanawida was there.

All of the Mohawk people were then convinced that this Dekanawida must have been sent by the Creator. They were convinced that this Dekanawida had the power to bring the Great Peace.

Near the Mohawks lived the Many Hill People, the Onondagas. They were afraid all the time. An evil monster-man lived just south of their villages. His name was Adodarho. His body was bent in seven directions and his hair was full of living snakes. He was a cannibal and could make magic to do evil things.

The Onondagas tried many times to get him to stop doing evil things but every time they failed. A Mohawk man helped them try: his name was Hayontawatha. (Sometimes he is called Hiawatha, but that is not right.)

In his attempt to solve the problem of Adodarho, Hayontawatha's seven daughters were killed by that man's evil magic. Hayontawatha's sorrow was so great that he left that country and wandered afar in search of quiet for his soul.

He said, "Men boast what they would do in extremity but they do not do what they promise. If I should see anyone in deep grief I would move these shells from this mourning pole and console him. The shells would become words and lift away the darkness with which they are covered. Moreover, I truly would do as I say." He meant that he would put aside the symbols of his sorrow, the pole and the shells, and turn his mind outward to others.

Hayontawatha wandered far, his mind made up that he would help people who were in grief. This he did. But no one seemed to want to help Hayontawatha in his grief.

He wandered far and at last found himself once again in the land of his People of the Flint Country, the Mohawks.

There Hayontawatha met Dekanawida.

Dekanawida said to him, "My Younger Brother, it has now become very plain to my eyes that your sorrow must be removed. Your griefs and your rage have been very great. I shall now undertake to remove your sorrow so that your mind may be rested."

Then Dekanawida made the Condolence Ceremony for the first time. It cleared the sadness from Hayontawatha and restored peace to his troubled mind. The Condolence Ceremony helped him so much that the people saw its worth and it is even now performed by the Iroquois people when it is needed.

A strong friendship sprang up between the two great men. This friendship was tied together by their desire to bring peace among the Iroquois people.

Dekanawida said to Hayontawatha, "My Junior Brother, your mind being cleared and you being competent to judge, we shall now make our laws and when all are made we shall call the organization we have formed the Kayanerenkowa, the Great Peace. It shall be the power to abolish war and robbery between brothers and bring peace and quietness."

It took a long time for Dekanawida and Hayontawatha to create the Great Peace. This is how they did it. Each village was already organized in a way similar to that of all the other villages. No matter what nation, no matter what village it was, the people living there belonged to various clans. Clans were large extended families whose members were all related one to another through the women. These clans were named for a related animal or creature. And each nation had three or more clans living within it.

There were at that time in the north five distinct nations: the Mohawks, the Onondagas, the Cayugas, the Oneidas, and the Senecas. Dekanawida's idea was to tie these Five Nations together with the bond of kinship. So it was that, from that time on, all the members of the Wolf Clan of each village and nation, for example, should feel related to all the other Wolf Clan members. The same went for the Bear Clan members and the Turtle Clan members and so forth and so on across the nations.

In this way, then, two kinds of bonds tied the Five Nations together: a vertical bond united people together as five single nations, and a horizontal bond tied people together between nations, across national boundaries, through the kinship of clans. This made for a strong union.

But the story of Adodarho, the evil monster-man, is not over yet.

The Mohawks, the Senecas, the Cayugas, and the Oneidas were all set to form the Confederacy. Yet it was important to have the Onondagas join if the Confederacy was to work. The Onondagas lived right in the center of these nations: to the west of the Onondagas lived the Senecas and the Cayugas and to the east of the Onondagas lived the Oneidas and the Mohawks. It was like a chain with the center link missing. It was like a long house with the central fire unlit.

And, too, it was important for the Onondagas to join the Confederacy because theirs was the largest number of people of any nation and they had more villages than any other nation.

But the Onondagas were afraid to join for one very good reason: Adodarho. They were afraid his evil magic would destroy them if they joined.

So Hayontawatha and Dekanawida went to see Adodarho.

They found him with his body twisted in seven directions and his hair full of writhing snakes.

They sang the Hymn of Peace to Adodarho to cure his crooked mind. Then Dekanawida rubbed his hand all over him to cure his crooked body.

Adodarho became straight in mind and body. All the evil fled.

The Senecas and the Mohawks were made the Elder Brothers of the League of the Iroquois. The Cayugas and the Oneidas became the Younger Brothers. And the Onondagas were, from then on, the Fire Keepers. Should there be an even vote between the Elder and the Younger Brothers, the Fire Keepers cast the tie-breaking ballot.

Other nations have occasionally been adopted into the Great League. The Tuscarora Nation became the sixth major member after the Christians pushed them out of their homeland in the early 1700s. Since 1722, the Confederacy has been known as the League of the Six Nations of the Iroquois.

Women's Nominating Belt · The women of the Confederacy hold the right to nominate its Lords from among their several clans. The belt verifies that a ⌐ ⌐on has been reached. Holder: New York State Museum at Albany

4. The League

The League of the Iroquois lives today as it has lived for hundreds of years. Each Iroquois is a member of his own nation—the nation of his mother. He is a Mohawk, an Oneida, an Onondaga, a Cayuga, a Seneca, or a Tuscarora. He is also a member of his own clan—the clan of his mother. He is a Wolf, a Bear, a Turtle, a Deer, an Eel, a Snipe, or any of a few others, depending on what clans his nation has.

The Chiefs, or Lords, who represent the people are elected. There are about fifty Lords altogether from the Six Nations. The positions of the Lords are hereditary in the sense that they have come down through certain clan families from the time of Dekanawida and Hayontawatha until now. When a Lord is chosen from his clan family, he is bestowed with the name of the original Lord of that clan family who joined in the Great Peace long ago.

It is the women who decide which of their sons will

become the new Lord in their clan family when a vacancy occurs. Together the women discuss the qualities of several possible male candidates. After arriving at a consensus, it is taken to the Clan Mother, the wise leader of the whole clan. If she finds agreement with them, she announces the decision of the women to the rest of the clan. All the clan members then vote for or against that person. And, ultimately, the Council of Lords must vote their final approval of the candidate, vote upon who shall wear the deer horns of a Lord of the people.

In this way, a democracy older than that of the United States is carried on and maintained. Before women were allowed to speak and vote in Europe and in America, Iroquois women were speaking and voting. Before everyone had the right to vote in Europe and America, all Iroquois people were voting for their representatives. Before democracy was practiced in Europe and white America, democracy was a way of life for the Iroquois.

Lords are chosen for their good character and knowledge of religious and civic things. Unlike the leaders of many other governments, Iroquois Lords are usually very poor. A good Chief *gives;* he does not *take.* A good Lord keeps his position for the whole of his life. If a Lord changes and becomes bad, he is dehorned by his Clan Mother and another person is found to fill that place. It is very shameful to be dehorned—to lose one's right to wear the deer horns of the Lords. It does not happen very often.

There are really three kinds of Chiefs who sit in the Confederate Council of the Iroquois.

We have talked so far only about the Lords of the Six Nations Confederacy. We saw how they are chosen from certain clan families in each of the nations. These, in a way, are hereditary positions, but chosen democratically even so.

Then there are Pine Tree Chiefs. Any man who shows special ability to work for the good of his people may be elected by the Lords to sit in the Confederate Council. It does not matter which nation he comes from or what clan he belongs to. It is his personal worth and his ability and willingness to help all the people of the Six Nations that determines his selection as a Pine Tree Chief.

Each Nation selects its own War Chief, the third kind of Chief. The War Chief is chosen in the same way that a Lord is chosen. That is, the procedure begins with the clan women, and so forth.

The War Chief's duties are to carry messages to and from the Lords and to take up arms when it is necessary to defend the people. The messages they receive and present to the Lords come from many places. They may come from governments or people outside the Six Nations or they may come from inside the Six Nations. If the Iroquois people are unhappy about a matter before the Lords, the War Chiefs deliver the opinions of the women on that matter to the Lords for their consideration.

The War Chiefs may sit in Council, may present matters to the Council, and may discuss matters with the Council Lords and Pine Tree Chiefs. But the War Chiefs have no vote. This is because the Iroquois do not believe that men of war should make decisions for their people. They believe that only men of peace should decide the future of the people.

And it is true that the War Chiefs have no power to say

when the Iroquois should go to war. Neither do the Lords nor the Pine Tree Chiefs.

It is the women who decide when the men will go to war because it is the women who will weep afterward. And more than that. It must be clear that the women, the Mothers of our People, are indeed very strong. It is they who choose the Lords, the War Chiefs, and the Pine Tree Chiefs. It is they who speak through the voices of their chosen leaders. It is they who have the power to de-horn. And, most of all, it is they who maintain and per-petuate the harmony of the people through the lines of kinship.

The Confederate Council of the League of the Iro-quois makes decisions on matters which affect all the Six Nations together. Anything which affects only an individ-ual nation's business is a matter only for that nation. Then the clan chiefs of that nation hold council and make decisions independent of the Confederate Council.

Thus it is that, in similar fashion, the business of a state in the United States is handled by that state alone; the business of all the states is handled by Congress. This is one of the lessons the Iroquois taught Benjamin Franklin and which helped him to write his Albany Plan of Union, the basis of the Constitution of the United States.

The Confederate Council of the League of the Iroquois meets on Onondaga land, as it was promised long ago to Adodarho by Dekanawida. Although all the Six Na-tions' languages are spoken in meeting, the main lan-guage is Mohawk, out of respect to Hayontawatha and the Mohawk Nation which was the first to join the Great League.

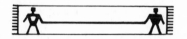

5. The Islands

The great island of Iroquois in the sea of Algonkians has been invaded and much of it lost during the last several centuries. Now there are only tiny islands of Iroquois in a sea of white men. The sea of Algonkians in the northeastern United States has all but gone dry. The little Iroquois islands are found in New York State, Pennsylvania, Ontario Province, and the Province of Quebec. There are also Iroquois in Wisconsin, Alberta Province, and in northeastern Oklahoma. These places are now the Iroquois homeland, no matter how small or dispersed.

The Canadian and United States census-takers have always found it hard to count Indians, especially Iroquois. But here are some population figures for the various Iroquois communities compiled during the 1960s.

MOHAWK

Oka, or Lake of Two Mountains Band, Quebec	507
Caughnawaga Band, Quebec	3,198
Akwesasne (St. Regis), New York, Ontario, Quebec	1,865
Deseronto Band, Ontario	1,601
Watha Band, Ontario	241
Six Nations Reserve, Ontario	2,600
Paul's Band, Alberta	123
	10,135

ONEIDA

Oneida Reserve, New York	369
Oneida Tract, Ontario	1,068
Green Bay, Wisconsin	3,472
Six Nations Reserve, Ontario	650
	5,559

ONONDAGA

Onondaga Reserve, New York	744
Six Nations Reserve, Ontario	400
	1,144

SENECA

Tonawanda Band, New York	688
Cattaraugus Band, New York	
Allegheny Band, New York	
Oil Springs, New York	3,188
Cornplanter Band, Pennsylvania	
Six Nations Reserve, Ontario	250
	4,126

CAYUGA

Cattaraugus Reserve, New York	237
Six Nations Reserve, Ontario	1,450
	1,687

TUSCARORA

Tuscarora Reserve, New York	452
Six Nations Reserve, Ontario	550
	1,002

OTHER COMMUNITIES

Seneca-Cayuga, Oklahoma	930
Iroquois Settlement, Ontario	1,780
	2,710

Altogether, then, there are about 26,363 Iroquois living in distinct communities in Canada and the United States. To count the number of Iroquois living outside these communities along with those listed above, we might say that there are approximately 50,000 Iroquois of the Six Nations in all. That comes to many times their number when the white men arrived in their country. The Iroquois are not dying out!

But while the population has rapidly increased, the Iroquois land base has rapidly decreased. The islands grow smaller and smaller. How so?

The reason for the land loss in earlier days was because of war with the French, British, and Americans. Some feel that it is right to take the lands of those who have been defeated in war. It is an age-old practice. When the Iroquois thrust themselves into Algonkian territory, they too kept the lands that they had won when founding their nations. Yet ever after that, it was Iroquois practice to leave their defeated enemies in possession of their lands and to make friends and allies of them.

From the time of the founding of the United States, Iroquois lands have been taken away piecemeal by many kinds of people and many different agencies. During the last twenty or thirty years, these land-takings have become very alarming since there is so little land left to take.

During the last decade in the United States, the New York Power Authority took Tuscarora lands, the St. Lawrence Seaway Authority took Mohawk lands, the New York State Highway Department took Onondaga and Seneca lands, and the U.S. Corps of Engineers took most of the Allegheny Seneca Reserve. Canadian interests have also whittled away at Iroquois lands in that country. And the taking has not stopped even now.

The Iroquois people are very naturally upset about this continual land-taking. It is difficult for us to understand how the United States government, for instance, can allow lands to be taken away when it was George Washington who promised us that the lands would always remain ours, ". . . as long as the grass shall grow and the waters flow. . . ." It strikes us that the government does not honor the Father of the United States as much as we do. That is very strange indeed. Our treaties north of the St. Lawrence River were made with the kings and queens of England. England's child, Canada, does not seem to respect the wishes of the kings and queens as much as we do. Why should this be? We do not know.

One of our everlasting problems is the business of Iroquois sovereignty. Or, perhaps, the problem is not ours, but Canada's and the United States'. The treaties we made with the Dutch, the British, the French, and the Americans were made between us and them as sovereign nations. We were equal to them and they were equal to us. In fact, in the early days, we were *more* equal than they because they were weak and we were strong. Now it is the other way around. But even so, the Six Nations of the Iroquois are a separate country from Canada and the United States, we believe. All the treaties recognized this. George Washington recognized this. Thomas Jefferson recognized this. John Marshall recognized this. And, even today, we recognize this.

So when the United States government took Seneca lands to build Kinzua Dam, we looked upon it as Spain would if France built a dam on her lands.

Our lands, though cut up on both sides of the St. Lawrence River, we see as one nation. To us, there is no border between the United States and Canada. There never was before, not until someone drew a line on a map. All our people are one people. There is no line between Iroquois. The Jay Treaty recognized this. It guaranteed that the Iroquois people could always pass back and forth over the white man's border without interference. But there has been much interference. Much. Why should this be? We do not know.

6. The Border Crossing

Many years ago, a Tuscarora chief said that the Iroquois
should show the countries of Canada and the United
States that we honor our treaties and that they should,
too. On the matter of the Jay Treaty, this Tuscarora chief
said that the Iroquois people should renew their faith in
the treaty and try to encourage Canada and the United
States to renew their faith in the treaty. And so now, every
year in July, a day is set aside for the Border Crossing
Ceremonies. Every year, the Iroquois renew the strength
of the Jay Treaty and remind the two Christian nations of
their treaty obligations.

The Border Crossing Ceremonies are both serious and
fun. The purposes of reminding and keeping the border
open are serious and the speeches of the important men
are serious. But all the rest is fun.

The Ceremonies begin with a parade. One year, the

parade begins on the Canadian side of Niagara Falls and the next year it begins on the United States side. The parade crosses over one of the bridges to the other side where it comes to rest at a park where everyone will spend the day having a good time.

Iroquois come from all directions to take part in the Ceremonies. And many other kinds of Indians come to help the Iroquois celebrate. There is a warm feeling among all people. There is much smiling being done. There is big laughter. That is good because the Iroquois think there are only two kinds of laughter: big laughter and no laughter.

The important men make important speeches and the people nearby listen respectfully. Farther away, the children run around and yell and laugh.

Many of the women get together to prepare food for everyone. But their work really began several days ago. Making bread and corn soup takes a couple of days for just one family; for many people, it is a long-time job. But now, it is only a matter of heating up the corn soup, making tea and coffee, and doing things like that. The women are making big laughter, too. They enjoy working together. And no Iroquois woman ever makes a small laugh.

The children run around near the women, around and underneath the tables and cars, and everywhere children can get. Once in a while a child will hurt itself from playing too hard. The child comes and stands quietly next to the mother until it feels better. A good Iroquois child should not cry out loud, only softly.

After some time, when the speeches get over, there is

dancing by different Indian groups and baseball games and lacrosse games. Although the Ceremonies are really for the Iroquois, many non-Indian people come to them, too. Mostly these are tourists since the local people have seen Iroquois often enough and do not need to see them more than they do.

The tourists think that the Indians are strange and colorful. The Indians think that the tourists are strange and colorful.

The tourists stare at the Indians and talk loudly to one another about the Indians, even when they can be heard by all. They point at Indian people. Often they ask Indians to stand still while they take their pictures. It is usually the children whose pictures they get. The older people work hard to be polite but they do not like to be shot at by tourist cameras. Neither do the children, really.

But it is such a good time for the Iroquois and their Indian friends that the bad manners of the tourists can be overlooked. There is no room inside for being unhappy at the Border Crossing Ceremonies.

You do not have to eat corn soup. You may eat hot dogs and things like that. But the best way to watch the young men play baseball and lacrosse is with a bowl of hot corn soup in your hand. Eating it, of course.

The reserves have baseball teams that compete. During baseball season, they travel back and forth to play one another. Several games are played at the Ceremonies. Some teams are made up of members all from one nation of the Iroquois. Some teams have mixed Six Nations teammates. A few even have Algonkians on the team. But the best games are when an Iroquois team plays an Algonkian team. These games make you remember that the Iroquois and the Algonkians used to be enemies. They play very hard and both sides want to win very much. When a game like this is over, everyone takes a deep breath and laughs it out. Those are the best games.

The reserves have lacrosse teams as well. It is very special to us. Lacrosse is dangerous, both to play and to watch. The people who are watching must be very alert, almost as alert as the players. They may catch the ball, too, even if they do not want it. It can hurt.

Lacrosse is very fast. Usually it is only Iroquois teams that play each other at the Border Crossing Ceremonies. Lacrosse is played all over the world and in the Olympics, too, but it was invented by the American Indians. The Iroquois believe that the Iroquois invented it, and with us it is sacred, as well. It is drama and ritual and sport all at once.

The day grows long and the July sun is hot. While the young men play baseball and lacrosse and while others are singing and dancing, still others are resting and sleeping in the shade. When the shadows become longer, there is more food ready for everyone. Fires are lit. People visit back and forth. Children do not run as fast now. They grow tired and slow. Sweethearts sit close to each other. An old man snores loudly once and everyone laughs. He wakes up a moment, smiles too, and goes back to sleep. The warmth of the air is also the warmth of good feelings that fill the people. If you listen carefully, far away you can hear Nia-gowa, the Great Bear, growling in his sleep beneath the falls.

7. The Long House

Iroquois may practice whatever religion they like. There
are many kinds of churches on the reserves, both
Christian and non-Christian. But whatever religion an
Iroquois selects for himself, something of the old beliefs
and the old trusts remain with him always. The religion
that grew up with the Iroquois from the time of their birth
as a people yet walks with them today. Sometimes the
Iroquois themselves do not sense that the ancient religion
walks with them, but it does. It can be seen in the way
people act and speak to each other. It can be seen in the
way they look at the stars and at the rainbow and in how
they hold the warm earth in their hands.

The ancient religion taught the people how to treat the
world in which they lived so that the world, in turn, would
treat them well. It taught them how to treat each other.
It was a quiet religion of beauty and love. It served the

Iroquois well. It answered their needs to know what lay beyond man.

The stories and legends that went with the beliefs and practices of the ancient religion helped the people find their way through the world. These legends guided them through dark places and light places in the history of the Iroquois people.

One or another of the legends carried the strange message that a giant white serpent would one day come to the shores of the land of the Indian people. The message said that the white serpent would cause enormous suffering and death to the people. It said that the white serpent would hold power over the people for a long time.

One day, white men came as a small wave to the shores of the land of the Indian people. At first the people welcomed them. But in time, people began remembering the message about the white serpent. The Iroquois for a long time held off the tidal wave of white men. They fought well and they made peace well. But the tidal wave could not be held off forever. When it came, it crushed the Iroquois. The ancient world in which the ancient religion dwelled no longer existed. All was dark.

In this time of darkness, many kinds of Christians came to the Iroquois. They wanted the Iroquois to share the ancient Christian religion with them. But even as the ancient world of the Iroquois religion no longer existed, neither did the ancient world of Christian religion. So thought the people.

Again and again the Christians came to the Iroquois. Some Christians were holy men. Most were not.

In the summer of 1805 there occurred an exchange of words which made clear the Iroquois view of Christianity at that time. It was Red Jacket, a Seneca chief, and the Reverend Mr. Cram, a Boston missionary, who traded these words:

Red Jacket welcomed all to the gathering:

"Brothers of the Six Nations; I rejoice to meet you at this time, and thank the Great Spirit, that he has preserved you in health, and given me another opportunity of taking you by the hand.

"Brothers; The person who sits by me, is a friend who has come a great distance to hold a talk with you. He will inform you what his business is, and it is my request that you would listen with attention to his words."

Then the missionary spoke:

"My Friends; I am thankful for the opportunity afforded us of uniting together at this time. I had a great desire to see you, and inquire into your state and welfare; for this purpose I have travelled a great distance, being sent by your old friends, the Boston Missionary Society. You will recollect they formerly sent missionaries among you, to instruct you in religion, and labor for your good. Although they have not heard from you for a long time, yet they have not forgotten their brothers the Six Nations, and are still anxious to do you good.

"Brothers; I have not come to get your lands or your money, but to enlighten your minds, and to instruct you how to worship the Great Spirit agreeably to his mind and will, and to preach to you the gospel of his son Jesus Christ. There is but one religion, and but one way to serve God, and if you do

not embrace the right way, you cannot be happy hereafter. You have never worshipped the Great Spirit in a manner acceptable to him; but have, all your lives, been in great errors and darkness. To endeavor to remove these errors, and open your eyes, so that you might see clearly, is my business with you.

"*Brothers;* I wish to talk with you as one friend talks with another; and, if you have any objections to receive the religion which I preach, I wish you to state them; and I will endeavor to satisfy your minds, and remove the objections.

"*Brothers;* I want you to speak your minds freely; for I wish to reason with you on the subject, and, if possible, remove all doubts, if there be any on your minds. The subject is an important one, and it is of consequence that you give it an early attention while the offer is made you. Your friends, the Boston Missionary Society, will continue to send you good and faithful ministers, to instruct and strengthen you in religion, if, on your part, you are willing to receive them.

"*Brothers;* Since I have been in this part of the country, I have visited some of your small villages, and talked with your people. They appear willing to receive instructions, but, as they look up to you as their older brothers in council, they want first to know your opinion on the subject.

"You have now heard what I have to propose at present. I hope you will take it into consideration, and give me an answer before we part."

As is proper, the chiefs and warriors discussed the words spoken by the Reverend Mr. Cram. Then their spokesman arose. Red Jacket replied to the Reverend Mr. Cram thus:

"*Friend and Brother;* It was the will of the Great Spirit that we should meet together this day. He orders all things,

and has given us a fine day for our Council. He has taken his
garment from before the sun, and caused it to shine with
brightness upon us. Our eyes are opened, that we see clearly;
our ears are unstopped, that we have been able to hear dis-
tinctly the words you have spoken. For all these favors we
thank the Great Spirit; and Him *only*.

"*Brother;* This council fire was kindled by you. It was at
your request that we came together at this time. We have lis-
tened with attention to what you have said. You requested us
to speak our minds freely. This gives us great joy; for we now
consider that we stand upright before you, and can speak
what we think. All have heard your voice, and all speak to
you now as one man. Our minds are agreed.

"*Brother;* You say you want an answer to your talk before
you leave this place. It is right you should have one, as you
are a great distance from home, and we do not wish to detain
you. But we will first look back a little, and tell you what our
fathers have told us, and what we have heard from the white
people.

"*Brother;* Listen to what we say.

"There was a time when our forefathers owned this great
island. Their seats extended from the rising to the setting sun.
The Great Spirit had made it for the use of Indians. He had
created the buffalo, the deer, and other animals for food. He
had made the bear and the beaver. Their skins served us for
clothing. He had scattered them over the country, and taught
us how to take them. He had caused the earth to produce
corn for bread. All this He had done for his red children, because He loved them. If we had some disputes about our
hunting ground, they were generally settled without the shed-
ding of much blood. But an evil day came upon us. Your forefathers crossed the great water, and landed on this island.
Their numbers were small. They found friends and not enemies. They told us they had fled from their own country for
fear of wicked men, and had come here to enjoy their religion.

They asked for a small seat. We took pity on them, granted their request; and they sat down amongst us. We gave them corn and meat, they gave us poison [alluding, it is supposed, to ardent spirits] in return.

"The white people had now found our country. Tidings were carried back, and more came amongst us. Yet we did not fear them. We took them to be friends. They called us brothers. We believed them, and gave them a larger seat. At length their numbers had greatly increased. They wanted more land; they wanted our country. Our eyes were opened, and our minds became uneasy. Wars took place. Indians were hired to fight against Indians, and many of our people were destroyed. They also brought strong liquor amongst us. It was strong and powerful, and has slain thousands.

"*Brother;* Our seats were once large and yours were small. You have now become a great people, and we have scarcely a place left to spread our blankets. You have got our country, but are not satisfied; you want to force your religion upon us.

"*Brother;* Continue to listen.

"You say that you are sent to instruct us how to worship the Great Spirit agreeably to his mind, and, if we do not take hold of the religion which you white people teach, we shall be unhappy hereafter. You say that you are right and we are lost. How do we know this to be true? We understand that your religion is written in a book. If it was intended for us as well as you, why has not the Great Spirit given to us, and not only to us, but why did he not give to our forefathers, the knowledge of that book, with the means of understanding it rightly? We only know what you tell us about it. How shall we know when to believe, being so often deceived by the white people?

"*Brother;* You say there is but one way to worship and serve the Great Spirit. If there is but one religion; why do you white people differ so much about it? Why not all agreed, as you can all read the book?

"*Brother;* We do not understand these things.

"We are told that your religion was given your forefathers, and has been handed down from father to son. We also have a religion, which was given to our forefathers, and has been handed down to us their children. We worship in that way. It teaches us to be thankful for all the favors we receive; to love each other, and to be united. We never quarrel about religion.

"*Brother;* The Great Spirit has made us all, but he has made a great difference between his white and red children. He has given us different complexions and different customs. To you He has given the arts. To these He has not opened our eyes. We know these things to be true. Since He has made so great a difference between us in other things; why may we not conclude that He has given us a different religion according to our understanding? The Great Spirit does right. He knows what is best for his children; we are satisfied.

"*Brother;* We do not wish to destroy your religion, or take it from you. We only want to enjoy our own.

"*Brother;* We are told that you have been preaching to the white people in this place. These people are our neighbors. We are acquainted with them. We will wait a little while, and see what effect your preaching has upon them. If we find it does them good, makes them honest and less disposed to cheat Indians; we will then consider again of what you have said.

"*Brother;* You have now heard our answer to your talk, and this is all we have to say at present.

"As we are going to part, we will come and take you by the hand, and hope the Great Spirit will protect you on your journey, and return you safe to your friends."

But the Christian would not shake hands with the Iroquois because he said that Christians should not shake hands with tools of the devil.

Christians and the Iroquois did not often shake hands in those early days.

Then came the time when it was clear that the ancient religion needed new things added to it to make it fit a changed world. The Creator used Skaniadario, Handsome Lake, of the Seneca nation, to inform the people of the new things to be added. The messages Skaniadario spoke were called *Gaiwio,* the Good Message.

It may be that the most important new teaching was how to treat with the Christians and with the things of the Christians. The messages spoken through Skaniadario said that the Christians had things of much evil for the Iroquois. These were shown as a flask of rum, a pack of playing cards, a handful of coins, a violin, and a decayed leg bone. Of these things, Hanisseono, the Evil One, said:

"These cards will make them gamble away their wealth and idle their time; this money will make them dishonest and covetous and they will forget their old laws; this fiddle will make them dance with their arms about their women and bring about a time of tattling and idle gossip; this rum will turn their minds to foolishness and they will barter their country for baubles; then will this secret poison eat the life from their blood and crumble their bones."

After saying this, even Hanisseono cried at his own cruelty to the Iroquois people.

It was then that the Creator told Skaniadario to tell the people that not all of the things of the Christians were evil. There were things that would do no harm to the people. The message said:

"Three things that our younger brothers, the white people, do are right to follow.

"Now, the first. The white man works on a tract of cultivated ground and harvests food for his family. So if he should die they still have the ground for help . . .

"Now, the second thing. It is the way a white man builds a house. He builds one warm and fine appearing so if he dies the family has the house for help . . .

"Now the third. The white man keeps horses and cattle. Now there is no evil in this for they are a help to his family. So if he dies his family has the stock for help. Now all this is right if there is no pride. No evil will follow this practice if the animals are well fed, treated kindly and not overworked. Tell this to your people."

There was one more message about the white man's ways. The message spoke thus:

"This concerns education. It is concerning studying in English schools.

"Now let the Council appoint twelve people to study, two from each nation of the six. So many white people are about you that you must study to know their ways."

Many are the messages sent to the people through Skaniadario. Together they are called the Code of Handsome Lake. It takes three days of telling in the Long House for the Code to be recited.

Instead of saying "church," the Iroquois speak of the "Long House." There are Long Houses on most of the reserves in the United States and Canada. There are different opinions about Skaniadario, but the native religion is everywhere called the "Long House Religion."

The Long Houses are built more or less alike. They are

large wooden buildings usually with twelve windows. Sometimes there is one door on the south side. Usually, though, there are two doors: one on the east side for males and one on the west side for females. Inside, at least two tiers of seats ring the whole room. The women and girls sit on the west side of the room and the men and boys sit on the east side of the room. There are two big woodstoves for heat, one on the north end of the room and one on the south end. The center of the room is an open space with some benches for the speakers and the singers.

It is here that we relearn the *Gaiwio* in September for harvest and in February for the turn of the year. It is here that our ancient ceremonies live again in their proper seasons.

There was a dark time when the ancient religion no longer helped the Iroquois in all his needs. Then came the *Gaiwio*. Not all the people took the *Gaiwio* into their hearts. Those who did not became Christians or Mormons or some such. Then there was a dark time for the Long House Religion. People had turned away from it. But now, in recent years, the Long Houses have once again become full. The young people have discovered what some of the older people had forgotten. The young people have found that the marriage of the ancient religion and the *Gaiwio*—the Long House religion—is for the Iroquois.

Akwesasne Belt · This belt was made to record the return of the Akwesasne (St. Regis) Mohawks to the Six Nations Iroquois Confederacy. The four lines represent rafters for strengthening a building, perhaps a long house. The Mohawks and the League would each become as rafters or supports to one another. Holder: New York State Museum at Albany

8. The Steelworkers

The messages delivered to the people by Skaniadario made it plain that the Great Creator favored the growing of plants and animals by the Iroquois. It was no longer a thing for only women to do; now, with the sanction of the Creator, the men could lay down their spears and pick up hoes without becoming less than men. Now, today, many of the people on the reserves farm, even if just a little.

Yet, for the young men there is still a place for warriors. There is still room for bravery.

The Mohawks were the first Indians to be steelworkers. It all began in 1886. A big steel company was building a bridge over the St. Lawrence River connecting Canada with the United States. The bridge was being built near the Mohawk Reserve called Caughnawaga, near Montreal. Some of the Mohawk men were hired to do work on the ground. Some of the white men had the job of putting up the big steel beams for the bridge out over the water. It was a very dangerous job. Very few men dared to do such a dangerous job perched high up in the windy sky over a roaring river far, far below.

But, every so often, these white men far out on the beams would sense that there was someone near them. They would turn around and it would be . . . a Mohawk standing there, looking over the white man's shoulder. The Mohawks would run up and down and over and across the beams as though on dry land. They wore no safety belts and they did not hang onto things as they went. They had no fear of the heights, no fear of the narrow beams to walk on.

The old men tell us that there are two reasons for this. The first reason is that, in the olden times, the boys were tested to see if they were ready to be men by testing them on their fear of heights. The boys would be told to climb the tallest pine tree they could find on a very windy day. If the boy climbed to the very thin top and could stand the wind blowing him back and forth all day, then he came back down a man. All the boys had to do this, had to pass this test. There were other tests, too, so maybe we should say the boy came back down the tree almost a man. The old men say that is one of the reasons the men have no fear of heights.

The other reason they tell about really is not a matter of being brave. They say it is a matter of how the Iroquois people walk. They say that Iroquois people walk one foot in front of the other, in a straight line. White people, though, walk like ducks. Their footprints show one foot out on this side and the other foot out on that side. Their path looks like two paths, not one, so they say. When the Iroquois walks across a narrow beam, he walks in a way that is natural for him. When a white man walks across a beam, he must put one foot directly in front of the other like the Iroquois. This is not his natural way and so his body is off balance. That is the difference, the old men say. That is the other reason the Indians do not have fear on the high steel.

Some years ago an official of the company building that first bridge wrote Joseph Mitchell a letter. It said:

"The records of the company for this bridge show that it was our understanding that we would employ these Indians as ordinary day laborers unloading materials. They were dissatisfied with this arrangement and would come out on the bridge itself every chance they got. It was quite impossible to keep them off. As the work progressed, it became apparent to all concerned that these Indians were very odd in that they did not have any fear of heights. If not watched, they would climb up into the spans and walk around up there as cool and collected as the toughest of our riveters, most of whom at that period were old sailing-ship men especially picked for their experience in working aloft. These Indians were as agile as goats. They would walk a narrow beam high up in the air with nothing below them but the river, which is rough there and ugly to look down on, and it wouldn't mean any more to them than walking on the solid ground. They seemed immune to the noise of the riveting, which goes right through you and is often enough in itself to make newcomers to construction feel sick and dizzy. They were inquisitive about the riveting and were continually bothering our foremen by requesting that they be allowed to take a crack at it. This happens to be the most dangerous work in all construction, and the highest-paid. Men who want to do it are rare and men who can do it are even rarer, and in good construction years there are sometimes not enough of them to go around. We decided it would be mutually advantageous to see what these Indians could do, so we picked out some and gave them a little training, and it turned out that putting riveting tools in their hands was like putting ham with eggs. In other words, they were natural-born bridgemen. Our records do not show how many we trained on this bridge. There is a tradition in the company that we trained twelve, or enough to form three riveting gangs."*

Those first Mohawk men taught other men of their nation. And then they taught men from the other Iroquois nations, as well. The Tuscaroras were good learners and now many of the Tuscarora men work in high steel in Niagara Falls, in Buffalo, and in many places farther away.

The Iroquois steelworkers have helped to build many famous things in the years since 1886. They worked on the George Washington Bridge, Rockefeller Center, the Golden Gate Bridge, and many other buildings and bridges. It is said that when the Empire State Building was being put up, all the white men quit when the tower part was due to be built. So the Iroquois men finished it alone, not afraid.

* From "The Mohawks in High Steel"; © 1949 Joseph Mitchell. Originally in *The New Yorker*.

Now the Iroquois workers in high steel are asked to go all over the United States and Canada to do this dangerous work. And sometimes they go overseas, as well, to places like Venezuela and Saudi Arabia.

So, in a way, our Iroquois men are still the brave warriors they have always been. We are very proud that their courage is as strong now as it ever was.

*Everlasting Tree Belt · Representing the Tree
of the Great Peace, this belt confirmed all the
laws adopted by the Great Council at Onondaga
at the time of the founding of the Iroquois League.
Holder: New York State Museum at Albany.*

9. The Ongwe Onwe

Driving along the knife-new highway, we look for the
turnoff to Tuscarora. From singing concrete, we lurch
onto blacktop and then dirt. We leave flashy morning sun-
light for dappling forest. From the plain, we rise up the
escarpment.

Up the hill, on one side of the road, smoke rises from
the chimney of an Iroquois-style log house with its new
white caulking between the horizontally laid trunks.
Across the road, the two-story farmhouse is sheltered
by a centuries-old oak tree. In its dooryard, a yellow and
green harvester is parked near a wooden wagon filled
with Iroquois flint corn. Indoors, at the combination
wood-and-electric stove, a college girl sifts wood ashes
used in making corn soup. She speaks Tuscarora to someone while the radio plays the latest song hits.

There is a knock at the front door (which hardly opens any more because no one ever uses it). In comes the agent for the State of New York with the goods. One treaty provision still kept is the yearly distribution of unbleached muslin to each member of the Tuscarora nation. Through time, the amount of muslin each person receives has become smaller and smaller as prices have risen.

The State of New York would like to stop this yearly distribution and settle with the Tuscaroras for a sum of money. The Tuscaroras prefer the man with the muslin. We do not need muslin and we might need money. But we need reminding every so often of how formidable we once were. It is good for us to see the man with the muslin coming. Everyone is happy all day. People repeat the funny things other people said to the man. We try to feed him but he won't eat with us. He is anxious to be done with his work.

Around the big dining table now sit many family members. All are of the same clan except the husbands. The steelworker tells the farmer about how it was to work on the Verrazano-Narrows Bridge. The grandfather, the chief, comes to the table and offers a Long House prayer in the Tuscarora language. Supper is rabbit pie, venison steaks, and frozen vegetables.

It is an early supper because it is Sunday and we must drive to Tonawanda for the Long House meeting.

The sun has set and the afterglow has almost closed down as we reach the Long House. Cars are parked all

around. Electric lights have been switched on inside. As
we walk to the door, we hear voices singing songs as old
as the Iroquois. Deer hoof rattles mark our footsteps as
we, in our American-style clothing, make our paths according to sex to where we will sit.

For a few hours, there is nothing but Iroquois. We relearn our history. The orators tell us of our past glories. In
our languages, they tell us of our past sorrows. Through-
out all, the compassion of the Creator has been with the
Iroquois.

And now, when the ceremonies are done, we can
emerge into an outside world not of Iroquois making and
yet we survive. For a most valuable gift given the Iroquois by the Creator through Skaniadario was then the
sanction and is now the talent for improving our world by
adding to it things of other people. "There is no evil in
this . . . ," said Skaniadario, if it is done without becoming
prideful. So most of our homes, our clothes, the things we
use, are from the outside world. Even, sometimes, ideas
are from the outside world, too.

But what makes an Iroquois different from all others
is his knowledge that he is *Ongwe onwe,* the Original People of the Creator. He is a trustee of all that his people
have ever been and have ever done. He is the custodian
of his people's past. In him lies the responsibility for see-
ing that Iroquois not yet born receive and carry onward
their heritage. This is not a handful of dusty feathers. The
Iroquois have forever been guided by the hopes and
dreams of all mankind.

Ne skenno, Ne Gaiwio, Ne Gasha Sa
Peace, Prosperity, Power, and Equality to All.

> *Niawe'skenno',*
> Thank you, you are strong

Gwa'oora